BEASTS OF BRAY ROAD

CHICKEN BLOOD

A recount by
Travis Clark
and
Tom Lyons

BEASTS OF BRAY ROAD: CHICKEN BLOOD

Copyright © 2021 Travis Clark and Tom Lyons

All rights reserved. No part of this may be reproduced in any form or without the authors' prior consent, except brief quotes used in reviews.

All information and opinions expressed in *Beasts of Bray Road: Chicken Blood* are entirely the author's and are based upon his perspective and experiences. He does not purport the information presented in this book is based on any accurate, current, or valid scientific knowledge.

Acknowledgments

It's certainly not an easy task for someone to discuss their encounter with cryptids. Thank you to those who found the courage to tell their experiences.

Out of respect for those who were involved, all of the following names have been altered as a means to protect their privacy.

Important Note

This book is the 3rd book in the series. I highly recommend that you complete *Beasts of Bray Road: The Accident* before you begin this book. It is available on Amazon.

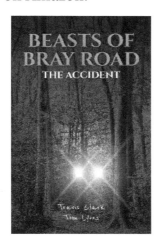

Contents

Chapter 1...1

Chapter 2...8

Chapter 3..13

Chapter 4..20

Chapter 5..24

Chapter 6..29

Chapter 7..35

Chapter 8..45

Chapter 9..54

Chapter 10..63

Chapter 11..69

Chapter 12..78

Chapter 13..88

Epilogue...96

Conclusion...101

Author's Note...103

Mailing List Sign Up Form.................................105

Social Media..107

About the Author 109

Chapter 1

An ounce of relief washed over me as the sounds of stampeding feet came past the closet and into the small bathroom connected to the left side of the bedroom. Knowing damn well that this might be my only chance, I jumped out of the closet and bolted down the hallway, internally praying that the main entrance had been left unlocked. My heart rate sped up as I observed that the door appeared to be shut. I didn't even turn around; I could both hear and feel the heavy footsteps not all that far behind me. When I grabbed hold of the doorknob, I first turned it to the right and pulled; it didn't open.

"No, no, no!" I gasped. But after I turned it to the left, I felt the brisk autumn air caress my cheeks. That brief feeling of hope got squashed when the large hand extended over my left shoulder and slammed the door shut before I could squeeze my way through. Without even a millisecond of hesitation, I wound up my torso and swung the bedframe leg at my abductor's face just as I would with a bat and a baseball.

"Aaaarrrrhhhggg!" the man shouted, immediately gripping the left side of his head as he stumbled a few steps backward. Before I knew it, I was out the door, running past the array of creepy targets, scanning the area for the first available gate within the abnormally high fence. Although I was getting closer to Keith's main house, I decided to take my chances with being spotted by anyone else who might reside there; with no time to hide, I knew I had no choice other than to rely entirely on my speed.

When I finally arrived at a gate that was off to the side of the main house, I was again disheartened when I noticed a heavy-duty lock securing it. For a few seconds, it appeared as though there was no hope to get out of there; however, that was before I heard the noise of boots running along the nearby terrain. There was something about that noise that pretty much propelled me over that fence. My determination to escape caused my adrenaline to pump so hard that I barely remember climbing over it. Before I knew it, I was dashing down the minor slope, back toward Henry and Denise's house.

First, I ran to the door that was closest to the kitchen, hoping that at least one of them would be nearby and could swiftly dial the police. The door was locked. Frantically, I tapped away at the window, hoping someone would hear it and rush over to unlock the door for me. Nobody came. There was no response of any kind. With little desire to look over my shoulder to check how close my kidnapper was, I dashed around the right side of the house, toward the garage where Denise had led me inside just a day earlier when I first arrived. The garage was closed. Frankly, it had begun to feel as though my demise was inevitable. Where was I to go if I couldn't even get back inside Henry and Denise's home? How had neither of them seemed to notice that I was fleeing for my life? Could it be possible that Keith Farley got to them first and then locked up their house? That potentiality had started draining any ounce of hope I had left, but then I twisted the doorknob of the front door, which happened to be unlocked. Having expected not to get in, I nearly fell onto my face after pushing the door open.

"Hello!? Denise!? Henry!?" I called out as I quickly rose to my feet and turned to lock the door behind me. I then waited for a few brief moments, expecting Keith's silhouette to appear behind the stained glass near the center of the door. But nobody came, at least, as far as I could see. I sprinted into the kitchen and brushed an old ceramic vase that rested atop a shelf around the left corner, causing it to wobble before it almost fell to the floor. Nobody answered my calls, and there was something about the atmosphere that felt exceptionally eerie. It could have just been my paranoia, but it felt obvious that something had gone down inside there while I was trapped at Keith's property.

On the other hand, no objects appeared to be knocked over, which didn't do anything to affirm the potentiality of a struggle. Additionally, Mickey was nowhere to be found. Because my memory had been so messed up over the last few days, I began to question again whether I had lost my mind.

Still hoping for my hunch to be inaccurate, I called out for the older couple once again—still, no reply. I hoped I was overreacting, and they had merely gone looking for me.

Chapter 2

Regardless of Henry and Denise's whereabouts, it felt like Keith Farley would come barging into their home at any moment. Even though all the doors were locked, the house just wasn't reinforced enough to prevent a relentless psychopath from breaking in.

While I ducked beneath the kitchen counters, listening for exterior noise, my eyes landed on the dirty backpack I had taken from the camper. I stood up and took a medium-sized chopping knife from a nearby kitchen drawer. It was one of the only ones with a hard-plastic sheath, deeming it the best choice for a weapon to place inside the backpack. I opened one of the cabinets and took the only nonperishable food items I could find, which happened to be made by Hostess or some comparable knockoff brand. I then opened the refrigerator and took what looked to be a fresh pack of sliced turkey. I didn't have much of a plan; all I knew was that staying put where Keith Farley knew to find me was the worst possible scenario.

After making sure I was equipped with enough warm layers and prepared for the unpredictable midwestern climate, I peeped around one of the corners at a window that showed me a large portion of the front yard. As far as I could see, there was nobody there. I then crept down the hallway and into the bathroom, where I had first laid eyes on Keith Farley and his home. With my eyes barely above the windowsill, I watched the area for a couple of minutes without spotting anyone.

No matter how much time passed, it seemed that I couldn't calm my heartrate; the idea that my abductor could be just on the other side of that wall, waiting for me to step out, was incredibly nerve-racking. I was so desperate for any sign of anything, any noise that would inform me that Keith was at a distance, or Henry, Denise, and Mickey were just fine. But the environment felt extraordinarily quiet, that kind of quiet where you could hear a pin drop. A large part of me wanted to stay put, but another part knew that that would make me a sitting duck.

Without further hesitation, I exited the bathroom and walked across the narrow hallway into the guest bedroom, where I had spent the previous night. After unlatching the lock on the window, I once again peered through the glass to make sure there was nobody within proximity. The frame was made of old wood, which made it a little challenging to push high enough to where I could climb past it. It seemed like the smarter idea to exit the house through a window rather than a door since Keith would likely expect me to do otherwise. I was nervous that I would get snatched up the very moment I landed in the yard, but, still, there seemed to be nobody in sight. I felt so vulnerable standing on that lawn that the only thing I could think to do was book it toward the forested area near the horizon. The idea of potentially getting myself lost all over again was most definitely daunting; however, at least, this would be a different section of woods from where I had ventured during my previous excursion. With a little bit of luck, maybe there were other homes not far off on the other side of what appeared to be very tall trees.

Without further ado, I began my dash across the vast open fields, only then recalling that I could be heading toward the pointy-eared, bipedal creature's territory.

Chapter 3

As I ran for cover, it quickly began to feel like the field was an endless abyss, especially seeing how the terrain was far softer than the grass-covered yard I had started from. I was reluctant to turn around; there was something about the thought of seeing that large, creepy man bolting after me that was too much to bear.

Although almost entirely out of breath, I felt relief when I somehow made it into the wood line untouched. I slid the backpack off my shoulders to further relieve my torso. With my hands resting on my knees, that was the first time I had turned around since fleeing from Henry and Denise's property. Again, it was nice to see that there was nobody there. I began to feel like I had somehow made it out of sight without anyone having seen where I was going. But if that truly was the case, why would Keith have seemingly halted his pursuit? After all, the guy *was* booking it after me just before I had climbed over his fence.

"Don't you touch him!" I suddenly heard Mom's voice shout at Dad as she followed him out the backdoor. She was wearing high heels, which made it difficult for her to keep pace with the guy.

As fast as I possibly could, I climbed the wooden ladder and entered the tree fort near the edge of our property. It seemed like the only place to run to, mostly because it was a little too small for adults to squeeze their way inside. In any case, our property was surrounded by a wooden fence that didn't provide any divots for climbing. Dad looked furious. What was I thinking by pulling on his leg like that and causing him to fall?

On the other hand, was I just supposed to sit there and watch him shout in my mom's face like that? He looked like he was only seconds away from hitting her. I couldn't just allow something like that to happen. But even though I had deterred his anger from her, that same rage was now locked onto me...and there was nowhere to hide.

Suddenly, movement from over near Henry and Denise's home caught my eye, snapping me out of yet another unpleasant memory. The distance was too great to tell for sure, but I figured there was a good chance it was Keith since it was a man without a woman or a dog by his side. At first, I felt confident that I was tucked far enough behind the edge of the woods that he wouldn't be able to see me, but when I saw him raise both hands toward his eyes, it became apparent that he was peering through a pair of binoculars. I practically dove behind the nearest thick tree, soon to stretch my reach for the backpack and quickly reel it in. I tried to hide every inch of my body behind the bark. There was something extra nerve-racking about spotting the guy with binoculars because I took it as a sign that he was likely still willing to pursue me, even if I had made it a reasonable distance away.

What was with this psychopath? What could he possibly want with a stranger like me? And what was with that female's voice I heard mumbling from the other side of that locked door? The more time that passed, the more prominent that mystery became. Although there was a part of me that was creeped out by that whole thing and wanted to get as far away as possible, another part of me wondered whether the individual had also been abducted by Keith Farley and needed help. By that point, it had become crystal clear that my only hope was to get to someone else's home so that I could call the police and tell them every aspect of all that had happened.

With caution, I steadily poked my head out from behind the tree, immediately startled by how much closer Keith was to my location. He was standing in the field, maybe a hundred and fifty yards away. It then dawned on me that I must have created tracks within the soil. Of course. How could I be so stupid? I should never have stopped running. After retreating behind the tree, I resumed my escape from an angle that I hoped enabled me not to be seen. Even though the man was trailing me, all I could do at that point was hope that he assumed I was further off than I was.

As I maneuvered my way through the dense ensemble of trees, I was grateful to spot a clearing not all that far ahead. I took that as a sign that the trees had likely been cleared out for another farming property. As I neared the edge of the forest, that feeling of hope escalated when I laid eyes upon a building in the distance. It was pretty far off, but it looked to be a sizeable barn, quite a bit larger than any of the structures on the properties I had just fled.

I was mere steps away from making my way out of the thicket and about to begin my dash toward the unknown property when, suddenly, I heard an unsettling noise racing in my direction.

Chapter 4

There was no mistaking what the noise was; it was the sound of a diesel engine, and it was powering its way over the encompassing unpaved terrain. I had this feeling that if the vehicle could fit, Keith would have driven straight into those woods and maybe even ran me over. Now unsure of how to proceed, I froze my stride so that I could listen carefully and try to determine how I should reroute my course. For a few seconds, it sounded like the truck had veered to the right and might be headed toward where I assumed the long stretch of underused road to be. But soon, I heard the engine returning to the vicinity, clarifying that it was scaling the outer edge of the woods. I then knew it was likely only a matter of seconds before the vehicle circled and came back into view. There was no way I would be able to make it to the building without getting caught. I was able to see a fence that would have at least separated me from the truck, but I still would have been in plain sight. All the psycho would have to do is park the car and hop the fence to run after me. As far as I could see, there was nobody around to help.

Without any further hesitation, I found myself running past the trees to my left, hopeful that the loud sound of

BEASTS OF BRAY ROAD: CHICKEN BLOOD

the diesel engine would soon begin to dissipate. My panic increased as the noise only seemed to grow louder, which made me feel as though I had been spotted. Doing my best to maintain my balance atop the leaf-covered, unpredictable forest soil, I began to veer to my right, hoping that I was at least headed somewhat in the direction of that building. If I could get close enough, maybe I could shout loud enough to get someone's attention.

But even though I couldn't see it, it wasn't long before it began to sound like the noisy truck was driving alongside me, tracking my every move. That feeling became more prominent as the engine seemed to slow in order to match my pace. Out of my peripheral, I could now see fragments of the large black truck through various gaps between trees. As far as I could hear, the driver wasn't saying anything, which made me worried that he could be steadying his aim and about to shoot me. It was one of those moments where nothing seemed out of the realm of possibility, and after the very abrupt sound of breaking glass, I would soon learn why.

Chapter 5

The combination of noise from glass getting broken and tires swerving made it clear that something unexpected had occurred to the strange man who had been chasing after me. Having caught another glimpse of the building I had spotted earlier, I decided there would likely be no better time to dash toward it. When I once again veered to my right and emerged from the wood line, I was nearly at the chest-high fence when I glanced over at the vehicle. What I saw stunned me and made me almost stumble and fall face-first on my way over the wooden barrier.

The glare from the sunlight made it so I couldn't see through the windshield, but I could see the large fur-cover legs hanging out of the passenger side window. They wiggled violently as the animal tried to climb its way into the truck but had some difficulty due to its size. Was this for real? Had this mysterious creature seriously just launched itself through the glass of a moving vehicle? Flashes of my father's tipped car suddenly surged through my thoughts. It now seemed even more possible that this creature was responsible for our accident. Just imagine a predator bold enough to pounce upon speeding vehicles. If that doesn't make you feel vulnerable, I'm not sure what would. I immediately noticed how its legs were shaped much more like a dog's rather than a man's. I don't remember thinking much of it at the time, but nowadays, I think that's one of the subject's most peculiar aspects. *How* and *why* would something with legs like that spend significant time in a bipedal stance? That seems to clash with many of our evolutionary perceptions.

It was kind of like witnessing a train wreck; I had to force myself to look away and continue to run toward the facility. Because of its awkward weight, I felt tempted to drop the backpack, but then I would also be sacrificing the knife, which was the one thing that might help me if the creature came after me next.

The closer I got to the facility, the more relief I began to feel. Still, I was hoping to hear or see anyone who might be able to help but, so far, no luck. Finally, I made my way onto the pavement that surrounded the long structure. I could hear a bit of commotion coming from inside, though I couldn't yet make out what was responsible. That was when I turned around to check on the status of Keith and the vicious creature.

From what I could see, nothing had changed since I emerged from the woods. The animal's lower body was still hanging out of the passenger side window while it continued to thrash around. Although I wanted to see how things turned out, I knew this might be my only chance to seek a helping hand. It was also best I got out of sight while both the creepy creature and strange man were distracted. It was kind of ironic how two entities that seemingly wanted me dead were now busy scuffling with one another. Given what I had already been through with those freaks, which one was more appropriate to root for?

It was right before I turned back around that I saw the wolf-like creature pull itself out of the vehicle and plop onto the grass below. What did that mean? Had it been injured? Or had it finished off Keith Farley and was merely looking for another way to get at its prey? Either way, something told me I shouldn't waste time trying to find out. I knew that if that creature truly desired, it was capable of catching up with me in an instant.

Chapter 6

On my way toward the door, I made my way past a couple of utility vehicles, similar to the ones I would see outside of the factory Dad worked at. They were in good condition, appearing as though they had been used recently. That brought me more hope that there were at least a few people around who could help me. As soon as I opened the door, my ears got hit by the racquet, and my nostrils hit by the stench. It looked as though I had

BEASTS OF BRAY ROAD: CHICKEN BLOOD

come across a sea of chickens divided by a walkway that ran straight down the center. There were no people within that massive room, only birds. About fifty yards ahead was another set of doors. I hoped that they led to offices where I would find an employee or two. While I ran along the path, the volume of the chickens seemed to escalate. I have no idea whether they were afraid of me or were excited because they expected me to feed them.

The first door was empty and dark and appeared to be nothing more than a storage unit for supplies. I tried the next door to the left and immediately locked eyes with an obese man with thin grey hair and glasses, who sat in one of those carts that you sometimes see immobile people using to get around. He held a pencil in one hand

and used the other to punch the keys of a calculator. Understandably, he looked extremely confused to see me enter the room.

"Well, now who in tarnation are you?"

"My name's Travis, and I'm being chased by a man and a—uh—maybe we should just call the police?"

"Whoa, let's just slow down a bit there, little fella," the man replied. "Take a deep breath."

I did as he requested and inhaled and exhaled.

"The name is Phillip, but most people refer to me as Farmer Phil. Now, what exactly is going on?"

"Look, I don't have time to explain, but there's a dangerous animal outside, and we should call for help before it somehow finds its way in here."

"Hold on a second," he said. "Does this animal you speak of have pointy ears and run around on two legs like a human?"

"Yeah, so you've seen it?" I said, excited by the idea that I could finally speak to someone willing to acknowledge the beast.

"Hell yes, I've seen it!" the man replied. "That thing was responsible for massacring a bunch of my chickens a couple of years back. Whatever that thing is, I thought I had scared it off for good."

"How?" I asked.

Farmer Phil had already wheeled himself over to a nearby cabinet, which he swiftly unlocked via a rusty, old combination lock.

"With this bad boy," he replied as he extracted a rifle from inside. "Haven't seen that animal in quite some time," he said, "and I'm not about to welcome it back."

Without further ado, the obese man rode his cart past me. I trailed him back up the walkway through the sea of chickens. "Look, I really don't think it's a good idea to go out there, or even to open the door," I said, somewhat hesitant to disagree with a stranger wielding a firearm. "Can we please just call the police to come out here?"

Farmer Phil didn't say anything. I couldn't tell if he hadn't heard me over the constant clucking or if he didn't care to respond. Either way, he continued toward the door.

"Is there anyone else here we should warn that the creature is on the property?"

"It's Sunday," Phil calmly replied. "I'm the only one here."

He used his thumb to tap a button on a small device hanging from a carabiner around his waistband. I felt the chilly autumn breeze graze my cheeks as the automatic door slowly opened, and Farmer Phil rolled on through it.

Chapter 7

It all happened so much faster than I ever could have anticipated. I don't think Farmer Phil's cart was even halfway outside before the beast pounced, knocking both the man and the heavy rifle onto the ground.

"Aaaaahhhhhhh!" Farmer Phil yelped as the massive jaws bit into the top of his head. Within a couple of seconds, there was so much blood that I wanted to vomit. I so badly wished for any way to help, but if you've seen one of

these creatures up close, you know
there's nothing I could have done. Since
the beast was right outside the entrance,
I didn't see any option other than to run
back inside. The chickens had become
noisier than ever, seemingly aware of
the extreme carnage unfolding just
outside the building.

The door to Farmer Phil's office
had been left ajar, so I dashed inside and
slammed it shut. I immediately
regretted closing it with such force, as I
was worried that it might have notified
the creature of where I fled.

The lock on the cabinet that Phil
had extracted the gun from was still
unfastened, but I quickly discovered that
it contained little more than boxes of
ammunition. I quickly circled the room,
my heart racing as I glanced over every

inch, looking for any means of protection. But the search came to a halt once I heard multiple chickens squawking. It was such a disturbing, bloodcurdling kind of noise that I knew it was attributed to none other than violent death. Although I felt terrible for the flock of birds, I was also grateful that they were there to buy me a little extra time.

It wasn't long before I spotted a vent on the wall near the ceiling. Given that there were no windows or other doors connected to the room, it became apparent that this was my only possible escape route. Luckily, I quickly found a screwdriver within a tray of old tools atop the desk. I had to stack a cardboard box onto the desk so that I could reach the vent. As I worked at unfastening the grille from the wall, I began to hear strange snorting and licking noises from the other side of the door, followed by what sounded like a chicken squirming throughout its final breath.

The proximity of the creature prompted me to speed up my twisting of the screwdriver. Suddenly, a loud bang against the door made me fumble the tool onto the floor, and I watched in horror as it rolled underneath a nearby shelving unit. As I reached my arm into the cobweb-filled space, the banging upon the door continued to speed up. I could tell the hinges were weakening and wouldn't last much longer. Seriously, it sounded as if something as powerful as a rhinoceros was attempting to make its way inside the room.

Once I was almost finished loosening the final screw, I grabbed the grille and pulled it from the wall. Fortunately, I climbed my way inside and progressed a good distance before I heard the office door fly off the hinges. My original plan was to crawl quietly to my escape, but the drastically increased urgency made that idea into a thing of the past. Every little movement of mine inside that ventilation shaft seemed as noisy as could be.

Although I refrained from turning around, I could see the faint light in front of me turn to darkness as the creature arrived at the vent's entrance. I felt saved; there was no way that an animal that large could squeeze its way into a space that narrow. I began to hear what sounded like the creature pacing back and forth within Farmer Phil's office, more than likely pondering what it needed to do to snatch its desired prey.

Soon after I made it around the initial corner, I arrived at another vent cover. This one hung above a dark restroom. The problem with that potential escape route was that there was no desk or anything below to break my fall. Additionally, it felt a little too close to the beast's location. I continued on my way. Up ahead, I noticed I had a choice of direction; I had to decide to proceed forward or to the left or the right. The initial plan was to take my time and explore multiple routes, but that was when I still felt safe. It wasn't long until I heard the unmistakable noise of the large creature stuffing itself into the ventilation shaft. Holy shit, it was actually willing to risk getting stuck in there in order to get at me. There was no more time to delay; I immediately propelled myself forward in the direction I was already facing.

As I rapidly crawled about on my hands and knees, the noise was dwarfed by that of the approaching heavy animal. Silently, I prayed that I wasn't en route to a dead end. Soon, I noticed a bit of faint light coming from around a bend up ahead. I had arrived above another storage room and immediately saw natural light, indicating that there was at least one window below me. As the animal's banging became louder, I knew that this might be my only chance to make it out of that shaft in one piece. Never mind the fact that this vent also led to yet another risky drop. The only thing that was keeping me alive was that it was undoubtedly a tight squeeze for the predator. Without that factor, it would have caught up to me ages ago.

I placed my back against the opposite side of the shaft and began kicking the vent cover. It barely budged. After a handful of fruitless attempts, I was having trouble deciding whether I should keep kicking or continue onward and hope that I came across a better opportunity to get out of there. The noise from the animal had become so loud by this point that it felt as though I couldn't hear my thoughts. By this point, the creature couldn't have been any less than fifteen feet away. The desperation to get out of there grew to new heights. Finally, I felt the sweet sensation of the vent cover detaching and plummeting to the floor. With barely any time to prepare my body for the fall, I slid through the opening, hoping that my already achy joints would endure the impact and allow me to continue onward. If I managed to break either of my legs, it would be only seconds before the beast was on top of me, devouring me alive.

I lost my balance when my toes touched the ground, causing my palms to absorb some of the impact. That was lucky because it probably helped me break my fall, thus, keeping my skinny legs intact. The floors were dirty with a combination of chicken feed and some other stuff that was likely used for gardening. The first thing I did was head toward the window. Immediately, I could tell that it hadn't been opened or even cleaned in years. I gave it a couple of seconds of effort before I concluded that it was rusted shut. I noticed several more windows in the room, but since they looked identical to the one I just examined, I decided to avoid them and head for the door.

As I put my hand around the doorknob, I heard the noise of the beast protruding from the vent.

Chapter 8

When I turned around, I immediately knew I shouldn't have. Seeing the creature that close was terrifying but simultaneously so captivating. It was challenging to look away because I was attempting to verify the nightmarish scene as reality. Though the light within the room was dim, it was bright enough to get a good look at the creature's eyes. I can't say why, but I had expected them to appear much more humanlike.

BEASTS OF BRAY ROAD: CHICKEN BLOOD

Perhaps I had subconsciously thought that a *werewolf* had been chasing me, and I had imagined the pair of pupils to help confirm that. I suppose what I read in Laura's journal could have contributed to the wild expectation.

As I stared at the vent, it felt like I was looking at nothing more than a scarce, wild animal, and a very ill-tempered one at that. That was also the first time I saw the long jaws full of razor-sharp teeth. Nearly every feature of the creature's head reminded me of an oversized wolf, except for the space between its ears. There was something about that area that reminded me of a hyena. It might sound a bit ridiculous, but it was kind of like the animal had a mohawk comprised of fur that was lighter than the rest.

Suddenly, it became clear that it would find a way out of the vent regardless of its size. Even if it were too broad to wiggle its way all the way through, I could see the thin sheets of steel starting to bend. It was only a matter of time before it found its way out of there and caught up to me.

Without further hesitation, I entered the hallway and slammed the door shut behind me. I looked to the right; maybe two hundred feet ahead, the dark path led to a T-shaped intersection. I then looked to my left; much closer in that direction was a door that had a small, square-shaped window. If it hadn't been for that tiny window, the hallway would have been pitch-black. The best part was that it appeared to be natural light, leading me to wonder if that door led to the outside.

As my mind scrambled to predict the most optimal route, the beast unleashed an odd-sounding wail. Something about that particular noise confirmed this was the creature responsible for the cackles I heard while lost in the woods. Instantly, the whole situation became even creepier, for it meant that I was indeed being stalked out there. What had prevented it from catching up to me out there?

The only conclusion I could come to was that it was satisfied with the fresh meat of the roadside stranger, and also the meat of...my father? What if *that* was the reason the predator was merely keeping me in its sights so that it could pounce once the cravings returned? No! I tried so very hard to dismiss such disturbing thoughts. Damnit, which way should I go? What if I only had enough time to test one of the directions before the beast came crashing through the door that was still only inches behind me? To the left, I went.

I was so glad when I arrived at the door with the tiny window and discovered it was unlocked. Assuming that the door would be much heavier, I ripped it open with such force that the doorknob slapped the wall and created a loud popping sound. Now it was likely that the animal would have no trouble getting right back on my trail once it broke out of the vent. That notion became even more unnerving when I learned that the natural light was coming from a window that was far too high and out of reach. It was essentially a dead end. The only other two options were a couple of restrooms: one for women and one for men. Damnit. What should I do? Should I take my chances by trying to hide? I peaked my head into the women's restroom (the closer of the two) and became even more nervous once I saw the size of the space. It was little more than a closet with a single stall and a small sink below a filthy mirror. If the creature were to corner me in that room, it would be mere seconds before the walls got painted red.

Without further hesitation, I dashed around the corner, back toward the initial hallway. After heading through the doorway, the combination of growling, screeching, and scratching prompted me to speed up. A brief moment after I ran past the door to the room that contained the beast, I heard what could only be the sound of its immense weight landing on the ground level. That was the noise that caused me to run faster than I ever had before.

Once I arrived at the T-shaped intersection, I heard the beast propel itself into the door. Chills ran down my spine as I then discerned the noise of the doorknob twisting, followed by the door swinging open. A cluster of what looked to be additional farming supplies beside a wall to my right influenced me to veer left. As I headed toward another windowless door, the charging bipedal footsteps not too far behind me grew louder and louder. Holy shit: please, God, allow this upcoming door to be unlocked. If it wasn't, my very brutal demise was only moments away. I would be trapped.

BEASTS OF BRAY ROAD: CHICKEN BLOOD

Are you enjoying the read?

I have decided to give back to the readers by making the following eBook **FREE!**

To claim your free eBook, head over to

www.LivingAmongBigfoot.com

and click the "FREE BOOK" tab!

Chapter 9

The good news was that the door opened. The bad news was that it didn't have a lock. I had just enough time to go through it and then push a nearby chair underneath the knob on the other side. The beast's immediate impact caused me to almost fall onto my ass before I could turn away.

It wasn't until I resumed running that I realized I was back in the very spacious chicken room. I was so focused on getting away from the animal that my mind seemed to tune out the birds' very loud and constant clucking. The nasty blend of blood and feathers was even more noticeable than I would have expected, given the minimal time that the beast spent inside the room before coming after me.

After dashing by Farmer Phil's office and then turning to head down the central walkway, the presumably plastic chair snapped, and the door sprung open. The beast seemed to growl in a way that insinuated it wouldn't allow me to get away this time. By this point, I had no clue what I could do to avoid the attack. Yes, the entrance door was still open, but what would I do once I was outside, even if I managed to make it out there before the predator caught up to me?

BEASTS OF BRAY ROAD: CHICKEN BLOOD

Farmer Phil's mangled corpse was still lying where he had died. I was preparing to leap over the carcass when I suddenly felt my feet slip out from under me. As I was falling onto my back, it was like I saw the whole thing in slow motion: the long arm equipped with razor-sharp claws swiped the air just above me. If I hadn't accidentally lost my footing at that exact moment, I would have lost half my face or perhaps even my entire head.

That gratitude from being spared was short-lived as drool dripped onto my hair and forehead. Lying on the ground, I viewed yet another seemingly slow motioned scene. Both the beast's snout and claws were headed directly toward my chest. My human muscles weren't capable of rolling out of the way before getting split open like a

Thanksgiving turkey. Suddenly, drops of blood splattered all over me; not only that, but the creature was no longer above me, and I was experiencing an intense ringing within my ears. What just happened? As far as I could tell, I wasn't dealing with any excruciating physical pain. I wondered if this was how the beginning of death feels. But I soon noticed a shadow approaching from the other direction. It was Keith Farley, and he was holding what appeared to be a small shotgun.

Fresh chills washed over me. There were a few moments where I waited for the firearm's barrel to align with my forehead. I figured this would at least be a quick and painless way to go, granted the psychopath permitted. But when I watched the man's hand extend toward me, I wasn't sure how I should react. Ultimately, it became clear that I was in no position to do anything other than to trust him. Keith helped me to my feet.

"Uh...thanks," I hesitated, still somewhat expecting some form of aggression. But the guy didn't say anything. Instead, he stepped around me. Discreetly, I turned my head to watch him. That was when I saw the mess. The beast was lying on its side, motionless. A large chunk that extended from its torso to its left hip was now missing, exposing a section of its broken ribcage. Its eyes were still open, and its jaws were ajar, giving the impression that it was as dead as could be. A part of me awaited the wolf-like shape to transform back into that of a human, but it didn't happen.

"Been wantin ter do that fer a while now," Keith suddenly remarked while standing over the carcass. The comment was far closer to a series of grunts rather than eloquent speech. By this point, I was so confused that I couldn't think of how to respond. I then looked at the space around my feet, soon to realize it was chicken blood that caused me to slip and fall. If it hadn't been for the beast savagely mangling several chickens and creating a gory mess, I wouldn't have avoided its attack. If it weren't for all that blood, Keith's appearance wouldn't have made any difference.

When the man shifted his gaze toward me, I felt my muscles flinch from preparation to run.

"Yer must not be one er them," he said before returning his focus to the carcass below.

Again, I didn't know how I should respond. What was the strange guy talking about? Was he insinuating that he thought I might be able to transform into a beast? It then dawned on me that Keith Farley perceived this creature as something more than just a mere animal. He thought this thing might be a werewolf.

"They don't seem ter want ter eat their own kind," the man muttered, still eyeing the mutilated animal.

"*They*?" I gasped. "You mean... there are more than one of those things?"

I don't understand why, but the man gave me a brief look that conveyed such a thing should be obvious. "Furs time killin one of em' bastards," Keith said as he kneeled to get an even closer look. The creature did appear to be dead, but it was probably the fact that I knew so little about it that I was tempted to warn the man to keep his distance. He was close enough to where the jaws would be able to take a chunk out of his abdomen had the animal possessed enough energy for one final attack. I concluded I should leave the grown man to do as he pleases, especially given how he came off as a loose cannon.

Soon, I thought I pieced together another part of this utterly bizarre puzzle. "Did you kidnap me because you thought I might transform into one of these animals?" I asked.

"Either that…," Keith began before a brief pause, "…or them neighbors of mine were about to feed you to em'."

I could feel my jaw drop. Was this man serious? Why on earth would Denise and Henry want to feed me to one of these animals? The chilly autumn wind seemed to intensify at that exact moment, brushing against my back as it whistled through the open doorway. Seriously, what kind of sick, twisted nightmare had I woken up to, literally?

"We better get somewhere safe," Keith then said. "Probably only a matter a time before the wolf's buddies come lookin fer him."

Chapter 10

"Shouldn't we do something about his body?" I asked after I watched Keith step over Farmer Phil's corpse and continue onward.

"Best we leave it," Keith said without turning around. "The man's remains might just buy us enough time ter get inside."

I felt sort of guilty walking off, but I was also glad to limit the amount of time I had to stare at the obese man's half-eaten head. I still have yet to come across a scene as revolting as that, even in the goriest of movies.

As I followed Keith to his truck, I noticed his outfit was torn in several areas. Somehow, he had managed to fight off the beast before it could squeeze its way all the way into the pickup truck. If it hadn't been for the vehicle's spacious interior, I don't see how the man wouldn't be missing half his head, just like Farmer Phil.

"Gun was put away in the back," Keith suddenly murmured as if he read my mind and knew I wondered why he hadn't shot the predator earlier. Keith's survival was another aspect where I lucked out. If it hadn't been for that, I wouldn't still be here to tell you about this horror story. Perhaps there is such a thing as destiny?

I felt somewhat tempted to bombard the man with questions, but I decided to wait until we made it indoors. Once I made it to the large truck's passenger side door, both Keith and I took a moment to use old hunting magazines to brush away glass shards from the worn leather seat. I couldn't help but notice splotches of blood on various sections of the interior, further affirming the notion that the middle-aged man was lucky to survive such a ferocious ambush.

As I entered the vehicle, my traumatized mind anticipated another one of those creatures to be approaching, but I was able to take a deep breath after perceiving that there was nothing around other than farmland and forest. My eyes then landed on a fabric patch that could be ironed onto an article of clothing. It read "U.S. Army Vietnam Veteran." Wow, was this guy involved in a war? No wonder he could survive the craziest of situations.

Once the diesel engine started, and we began to move, I was overcome with gratitude for how I was still alive; not only that, but I was still in one piece. But it was after Keith did a U-turn and we were on our way back toward his property that I remembered the woman's voice coming from the other side of the locked door. Whoever she was, it didn't sound like she was in stellar condition. Again, my curiosity almost got the best of me, but my gut told me to keep my mouth shut.

What if this guy, who I was currently sitting a few feet away from, was genuinely insane? What if that mysterious woman was connected to some vital secret that Keith didn't want me to know about? What were the chances that I would ever make it out of there? After taking another moment to gaze in all directions, I recognized I had no clue which direction I would need to run to arrive at another neighbor's home. In addition to all of that, it was apparent that this strange man was well-trained with weapons. I wanted to do everything possible to avoid not only being hunted by these wolf-like creatures...but also by a trained soldier.

I decided it was best to play it as cool as possible by seeming grateful for the rescue, at least until I figured out the truth of everything that was going on.

For all I knew, the simplest thing might cause Keith to flip out, and he would toss my ass right back into captivity. I needed to convince him that he could trust me.

Chapter 11

The mysterious man stepped out of the vehicle and waved his hand to invite me inside. He had his back turned toward me, and I realized this was another chance to run away. I had two choices: either I could follow him into a potential trap, or I could sprint right back into the woods and risk being tracked by more bipedal, dog-like predators within an unpredictable climate. Perhaps the latter was indeed the riskier option.

I trailed the man by a good thirty feet on the way to what I presumed to be his primary dwelling. He left the door ajar for me; I distinctly remember how the lack of interior light made it appear as though I was about to walk into a realm of darkness. Of course, I had no clue as to who or what kind of oddities could be awaiting my approach, but when I heard another one of those creepy cackles echo from a distance, I quickened my stride.

The home reeked of an old musty scent. It wasn't anything revolting but rather hinted that Keith was quite the hermit. All of the blinds were closed, and the only ounce of light was coming from an old television that I could see a portion of from the room ahead. What appeared to be some war program was playing without sound. I got the sense that the man might have muted the TV while spying on the outside, trying to ascertain whether it was a good time to come after me. Where was Keith now? I had become so focused on making sure I didn't knock anything over that I lost sight of the burly guy.

"Hello?" I called out awkwardly, unsure of how loud I should speak. Nobody answered. I thought that maybe he had gone straight to the bathroom to tend to his wounds. I didn't know what else to do other than to head for the room with the TV. The television provided just enough light for me to notice some of the contents displayed within a wood and glass cabinet. It was a collection of medals, antique weapons, postcards, etc., most of which appeared to have affiliations with Keith's tour in Vietnam.

For whatever reason, my eyes were most attracted to the postcards. I suppose I was curious to learn how others had interacted with the mysterious man. Right away, I could tell that people had once thought very fondly of the guy. The writer of one of the messages even stated how they missed speaking to Keith every morning at breakfast. Even though I was so young, the tone of these letters took me by surprise. It felt as though they were written for an entirely different character who also happened to go by the name of *Keith Farley*.

Suddenly, I heard the front door swing open. The noise from it slamming into the wall, followed by a gust of wind, made it apparent that I hadn't closed it all the way after stepping inside. The idea of one of those animals rushing into

BEASTS OF BRAY ROAD: CHICKEN BLOOD

the house through the open doorway prompted me to run over and shut the darn thing. But when I made it over to the opening, something caught my eye; a younger man in a police uniform was wandering around Henry and Denise's property. It was Officer Williams. His body language conveyed that he was searching for someone. *Holy shit, he must be looking for me*, I thought. I didn't hesitate. Before I knew it, I was halfway down Keith's hill, flailing my arms. I made sure to stay silent throughout my approach, as I didn't want to inform Keith of what was happening. Once I got closer to the officer, I saw that he looked mystified.

"Hellow again, kiddo, what were you doing over there?" Officer Williams said, his tone insinuating it was an unsafe place to venture.

"Keith, the guy who lives in that house, he kidnapped me," I said while attempting to catch my breath. "He crept up on me while I was in the barn." I didn't know how else to handle all of the oddities that were going on at once. Sure, I was incredibly grateful for Keith saving my life by shooting the creature dead, but that didn't eradicate my skepticism regarding everything else he could be up to. He seemed like a crazy character that should be investigated by the police to expose the extent of everything he was involved with.

"What happened to the Bennetts?" Officer Williams said. He seemed nervous like he could already tell something was very wrong. Even though he now lacked confidence, it didn't matter so much to me. I was just so thankful to be in the presence of an authority figure. All he would have to do is radio for backup, and police would be arresting crazy Keith Farley in no time.

I continued to observe the man's body language, waiting for him to take control of the situation, but it started to seem like he was even more freaked out than me. Could it be that, for whatever reason, this man feared Keith Farley? Officer Williams opened his mouth like he was about to speak but then turned and began walking around the side of the Bennetts' house.

"Wait, where are you going?" I called out. But he didn't reply; he just kept walking as though he didn't hear me. As confused as ever, I followed his lead. Officer Williams turned the next corner, apparently heading for the front door. As I continued to follow him, I glimpsed the man's vehicle parked in the driveway. It wasn't a police car. At the time, I brushed it off, assuming that perhaps the man had just gotten off work but hadn't yet had a chance to change out of his uniform.

Officer Williams opened the front door and closed it behind him. It was like he was so distracted that he forgot I was right there, trying to get his attention.

"Henry? Denise?" I heard the nervous man call out as I reopened the door and stepped inside. There was no answer. His face now looked sweaty. *What the heck is with this guy*? Even at my young age, I knew this wasn't how police officers are trained to react.

"Officer, I think you should call for help," I said. "I'm pretty sure Keith

Farley has an innocent woman locked inside one of the rooms of his smaller house. Who knows what he's planning to do to her? Someone should get her out of there right away." I was so concerned with the current, more urgent matters that I neglected to ask for updates regarding the car accident. In any case, Officer Williams seemed too spooked to discuss much of anything.

"Can't you please call for more police to come out here?" I asked, my tone conveying increasing frustration. The man didn't answer; he just kept pacing and pondering how to approach the current situation.

"Never mind, I'll just call 9-1-1," I said, grabbing the nearest telephone. It was only a moment before the man swatted the device from my grasp.

Chapter 12

I looked up at Officer Williams. "What'd you do that for?" I said, now realizing there was even more wrong with everything than I had possibly imagined. I'll never forget how sweaty the man's face was. He seemed so friendly when I first met him; now, he seemed like a deranged lunatic, quite possibly even less stable than Keith.

"I need you to tell me everything you saw while in that prick's house," Williams demanded. He was towering over me, seemingly ready to choke me out if I didn't cooperate. All I could think to do at that moment was run. The man blocked me from fleeing in any direction other than through the kitchen behind me.

"Hey! Get back here!" the nervous wreck of a guy yelled as he stormed after me. After dashing by the refrigerator, I ran around a corner and arrived at a narrow staircase. Fortunately, Williams lost his footing and tumbled down the steps; his figure barely missed me as I arrived at the lower level. I can't tell you how relieved I was when I spotted a door up ahead next to a small window exposing natural light. I had made it three-quarters of the way up the cement steps outside when I felt a hand grab the back of my jacket.

"Help!" I yelled as I gripped the railing and attempted to kick the man off of me. "HELP!"

The guy had only just managed to pull me closer and put his hands around my neck before I felt his grip slip away.

"Get off me, you bastard!" Officer Williams yelled. I looked up and saw the man getting punched in the face over and over. Yet again, Keith Farley had come to my rescue. Appearing to have little to no hand-to-hand combat experience, Williams flailed his arms, unable to deliver a single impactful punch. The hysterical man seemed to be losing energy by the millisecond. Soon, Keith put his opponent in a chokehold and held him like that until he passed out.

"Um, thank you," I said, picking myself up from the steps. Keith didn't respond right away. I could tell he was questioning why he even bothered helping someone like me, someone who refused to trust him.

"That rat ain't a real cop," he eventually muttered before lifting Williams from the ground and tossing him over his shoulder. "Wanna show ya something."

I took a few moments to ponder everything before deciding to follow his lead. I noticed Keith didn't turn to see if I was trailing him on the way back to his house, which was comforting because it indicated he didn't care to chase me; I was free to do as I please. But what the heck was it that this man could want to show me? I decided that I better obtain a little more clarification before I step back into that dark house of his.

"Excuse me, sir?" I said as I jogged several steps to catch up to him. "Isn't it best if we just call the actual police now?"

"First, I want ya to see I was tellin ya the damn truth," Keith commanded. His tone conveyed that he was tired of people not giving him the benefit of the doubt. "Them Bennetts *were* going to feed ya to one of them monsters."

"But why would they want to do something like that?" I said.

"Because they believe their son, Eugene, is one of them, and feedin him is the only way to maintain some kind of relationship with him."

"Huh? You're trying to tell me that Denise and Henry believe their kid is now a werewolf? How old was he?"

"Reckon he was about thirty. Eugene was obsessed with them monsters, always tryin to come up with new ways to lure them in. I lost my dog because of that boy's goddamn reckless actions. Anyhow, there came a day where Eugene disappeared. His parents believe he turned into one of them, while I'm near damn sure he was taken and eaten. But them nutjobs seem to believe their boy is now one of them so wholeheartedly that it even got me wonderin whether it might be possible. When I saw them welcomin you into their home, I couldn't be sure if you were part of their crazy cult or if they were plannin to use ya as bait. I suspected the latter. Either way, I needed to get you out of there before I could apprehend them. I wasn't about to let there be another victim. My conscience can't take no more of that, no sir."

"Well, what's with Williams?" I asked. "Why does he participate in any of this?"

"This here is Denise's younger cousin," Keith replied. "I ain't positive why he wants to be involved, but I've seen him show up to the property in a police uniform on more than a couple of occasions before I did some digging and realized he's no real officer. My hunch is that them Bennetts have him do that when they have a guest whom they'd like to give some reassurance."

"So, you're saying they do this sort of thing regularly?" I muttered.

BEASTS OF BRAY ROAD: CHICKEN BLOOD

"I'm not sayin it's an everyday thing," Keith said, "although, I'm near certain they would make it one if it were possible."

"But how do they even come across these people to lure into their trap? I'm not the only one to get lost in these woods?"

"I'm not positive how they come across all them victims, but the girl that I recently rescued was out of her mind when I got her out of there. There's no question they gave her some tranquilizer. If I had to guess, I'd say they slipped it into something she ate or drank."

My mind flashed back to when Denise offered me the lemon bars. Could there have been something in there that would have made me incoherent? Thank

God I turned down the offer. I had eaten plenty of their other food and felt just fine, as far as I could tell. Maybe the Bennetts thought they didn't need to bother with drugging me because I displayed a willingness to stay there until we received updates on my father? Perhaps my age had something to do with it. Who could say?

"The girl was also so bloated I thought she might pop," Keith continued. "Them Bennetts had been overfeeding the poor thing. I can't help but think they planned to fatten the girl up before the feedin. She's now recoverin in my guesthouse. I don't yet know the whole story bout what led to her capture, but she's already dealin with trauma, that's for damn sure."

"The Bennetts didn't try to come after you for taking her away?" I said.

"Until today, they didn't even know for sure I had their precious bait. And they know better than to come snoopin around my property. And they're probably not too concerned by the other potentiality that the girl had run off. Her mind was so out of whack that I bet they assumed she wouldn't make it very far before their supposed beast of a son caught up with her. Denise and that hound of hers might've been searchin for scraps of the girl before crossin paths with you."

Suddenly, I felt like I had put two and two together. "What's the girl's name?"

"Her name is Laura," Keith said.

Chapter 13

It's strange how the possibility that Laura (the author of the journal) was the one inside that room never occurred to me. For some reason, I thought I had heard the voice of an adult woman. I suppose that could have been because the series of events brought her to an inebriated state, thus altering her voice to a degree. Admittedly, I was pretty stressed at the time, which probably influenced my interpretation of everything happening within the environment.

While I was deciding what to ask next, Keith resumed his stride into his home. "Maybe you have your doubts," he called out from inside, "but I'll prove it to ya right now."

I looked over my shoulder to survey the land one more time before following the man back into his dark house. It wasn't long before we were standing in a basement lit by a single bulb hanging from an unfinished ceiling. The air felt damp and cold. The concrete floor was riddled with stains that had likely been caused by occasional flooding. I had only a moment to survey the area before I noticed Keith's energy had changed. Something wasn't right. His eyes were fixed on a door that had

BEASTS OF BRAY ROAD: CHICKEN BLOOD

been left ajar. He then placed Williams's body on the ground and withdrew a knife from his waistband.

"What is it?" I murmured.

"Shh!" Keith immediately commanded as he stepped toward the doorway. Once he was a mere couple of feet from the door, he barged his way in, fully prepared for another scuffle. It quickly became clear that the room was empty, and I could see a couple of old chairs near the floor's center.

"Them bastards escaped," Keith muttered just loud enough for me to hear. "Had the two of them Bennetts tied up down here. Was gonna force them to explain everything they had gotten up to. Then I figured I would let ya hear all of it so that you'd no longer look at me like I'm some nut."

BEASTS OF BRAY ROAD: CHICKEN BLOOD

Something about his words made me feel incredibly awkward like he knew I had been judging him since the very second that I first saw him. It even made me briefly disregard the notion that this couple of psychopaths were on the loose and might be looking for some retribution. "What about their dog, Mickey?" I said.

"Brought the hound to the stable and tied him up," Keith said, quietly, in a tone that conveyed understanding over my concern for an innocent animal.

With his knife still drawn, Keith had me follow him back up the stairs. Even if all of these people were utterly insane, I was at least grateful to have the more physically capable one temporarily on my side. Although he was trying to be careful, Keith's hefty weight caused each wooden step to creak. His body language suggested he expected an ambush at any given moment.

Soon after we reached the top of the steps, Keith ushered me to go in front of him so that I would be between him and the doorway. We were on our way to the door when, suddenly, a man came charging in from around the corner. It was Henry. He was shouting like a madman, and his hands were extended out in front of him, indicating that he was going for Keith's neck. With little effort, Keith caught the crazy man's wrists before they could reach his throat, but that first move turned out to be nothing more than a mere decoy.

"Look out!" I yelled after I watched the silhouette quickly rise from behind the sofa. It was Denise. Keith only had enough time to turn around halfway before the crazy lady jammed the small ax into the side of his head, splitting his ear down the center. Keith's eyes went wide as he died instantly. With the object still lodged in his skull, there was a heavy crash as his body fell face-first onto the floor.

That moment where Denise and I glared at one another is something I'll never forget. The room's lighting was dim, but it was bright enough for me to see the insanity in her eyes. It was just like how she looked when I found her staring at me from above the bed, only intensified. Without any further hesitation, I reached for the doorknob and exited the house. I had no idea what I might encounter on the outside, but at that moment, anything seemed safer than remaining inside that house.

As I sprinted down the slope toward Keith's gate, I could hear the noise of the old couples' boots about twenty feet behind me. I had no plan other than to try to outrun them. It was once I arrived at the gate that I couldn't believe my eyes. A police car was approaching from the Bennetts' lengthy driveway. I began waving my hands in the air, hoping to God this wasn't just another imposter of a cop.

I was so young and inexperienced that I had no idea the cops respond if you dial 9-1-1 but don't get a chance to speak to anyone. I had had just enough time to punch in those three digits on the Bennetts' telephone before Williams swatted the object out of my hand. I was so disturbed by his violent manner that I wasn't even sure whether I had dialed the number.

After making it through the gate, I began waving my hands in the air to make sure they saw me. Not one but two officers exited the vehicle and rushed over to greet me. When I turned around, Henry and Denise were no longer in sight. After informing both the male and female officer that I was indeed running for my life, the male officer took out his gun and ran in the direction that he saw the Bennetts run. The female officer radioed in for backup, and it wasn't long before law enforcement swarmed the scene.

Epilogue

It turned out that it *was* both Laura and her father who Keith Farley had rescued from the Bennetts' grasp. The two of them were locked up in that guesthouse room so that the crazy old couple would have no way of accessing them had they found out their nosy neighbor was the one who stole them away. I only caught a glimpse of the girl and her father as the police and medical personnel escorted them out of the house, but I remember thinking the

BEASTS OF BRAY ROAD: CHICKEN BLOOD

shape of their bodies looked very unusual. And they both had extremely puffy faces. If the Bennetts had been planning to feed them to their alleged wolfman of a son, it would have made sense why they looked like that. Perhaps that crazy old couple was doing something to fatten them up. Both Laura and her father were muttering gibberish during the walk to the emergency vehicles. Whatever it was exactly that happened to them, it was plain to see that it was rather traumatic. Thank the heavens that the three of us had a war vet nearby who cared enough to help. If it weren't for Keith Farley, I don't think any of us would still be alive.

I got in touch with my mother at the police station, and it wasn't long before we were reunited. I'm sorry to say nobody ever found my father, and, supposedly, there's no official conclusion regarding what happened to him.

Of course, I told my mother every detail of everything that had happened. Although she didn't seem to believe several aspects, I was confident that it was only a matter of time until the media interviewed me about this insane story that involved creatures that resembled werewolves. Those interview requests never came. It wasn't until I became much older that I started searching the internet for news stories about my experience. There were none. It was so frustrating to learn the harsh truth that authority figures prevent these kinds of incidents from reaching the public eye. Additionally, it felt like salt on the wound that I didn't have any way of getting in touch with Laura or her father. To this day, I have utterly no clue what their real names are.

Although most of my memory seemed to return, I never regained any perspective regarding what caused the accident. Not a day that goes by where I don't wonder whether I'm about to recall the details of how that nightmare began.

If, by some crazy chance, someone has told you about this same event, please reach out to Tom Lyons as soon as possible. I would love to speak with either Laura or her dad.

BEASTS OF BRAY ROAD

BEASTS OF BRAY ROAD: CHICKEN BLOOD

Conclusion

Thanks for reading *Beasts of Bray Road*! If you're looking for another series to sink your teeth into, you'll love *LIVING AMONG BIGFOOT: FIRST CONTACT*. The eBook is FREE for a limited time!

BEASTS OF BRAY ROAD: CHICKEN BLOOD

Author's Note

Before you go, I'd very much like to say "thank you" for purchasing this book.

I'm aware you had an endless variety of bigfoot-related books to choose from, but you took a chance on my content. Therefore, thanks for reading this one and sticking with it to the last page.

At this point, I'd like to ask you for a *tiny* favor; it would mean the world to me if you could leave a review on this book's Amazon.com page.

Your feedback will aid me as I continue to create products that you and many others can enjoy.

BEASTS OF BRAY ROAD: CHICKEN BLOOD

Mailing List Sign Up Form

Don't forget to sign up for the *Living Among Bigfoot* newsletter list. I promise this will not be used to spam you, but to ensure that you will always receive the first word on any new releases, discounts, or giveaways! All you need to do is visit the official *Living Among Bigfoot* website and click on the "FREE BOOK" tab!

www.LivingAmongBigfoot.com

BEASTS OF BRAY ROAD: CHICKEN BLOOD

Social Media

Feel free to follow/reach out to me with any questions or concerns on either Instagram or Twitter! I will do my best to follow back and respond to all comments.

Instagram:

@living_among_bigfoot

Twitter:

@AmongBigfoot

BEASTS OF BRAY ROAD: CHICKEN BLOOD

About the Author

A simple man at heart, Tom Lyons lived an ordinary existence for his first 52 years. Native to the great state of Wisconsin, he went through the motions of everyday life, residing near his family and developing a successful online business. The world that he once knew would completely change shortly after moving out west, where he was confronted by the allegedly mythical species known as Bigfoot.

You can email him directly at:

Living.Among.Bigfoot@gmail.com